I0426988

CONTENTS

INTRODUCTION

Welcome to the exciting world of advanced DNS technology. Ok, it's not really exciting, but we're going to pretend that it is because a little humor makes reading an entire book on a single feature a tad easier. We'll cover an important, yet often overlooked, part of DNS - Response Policy Zones, or RPZ. Ready to begin our journey?

WHAT ARE RESPONSE POLICY ZONES (RPZ)?

Response Policy Zones are a feature within BIND, the most widely used DNS software on the Internet, and some other DNS implementations. (Note: ISC, the guys who write BIND, have made RPZ freely available, but it is not an Internet standard[1], which means it can be changed at any time.) Different software may have different features or be configured differently, so always check the documentation for implementation you're using.

RPZ gives network administrators a way to customize how their servers respond to certain requests. In simple terms, RPZ let you create your own rules for how your server should answer different types of queries, rather than just passing on what it's sent.

RPZ has also been referred to as a "DNS firewall" or "DNS sinkhole" because it allows an administrator to control the flow of traffic to undesirable destinations by effectively hiding the IP Address from users.

---

[1] A several drafts of a standard have been written, with the latest, draft-ietf-dnsop-dns-rpz-00, having been written and expired in 2018. It can be accessed at via this link - https://datatracker.ietf.org/doc/draft-ietf-dnsop-dns-rpz/

Why is RPZ Important?

In our modern world where we're all connected via the internet, security is crucial. With cyber threats constantly changing and becoming more sophisticated, it's critical we have safe and secure ways to navigate and communicate online. That's where RPZ come in.

RPZ can improve security by allowing network administrators to control DNS responses better. For example, they can use RPZ to block access to harmful websites or redirect requests from specific IP addresses, reducing the risk of attacks.

RPZ also help manage internet traffic effectively within networks. Administrators can use them to direct traffic away from busy routes or towards preferred servers—improving overall network performance.

One of the more nuanced uses of an RPZ is to override single records for different zones. This can be very helpful in a variety of situations where you want to direct traffic differently without altering the entire zone file or maintain host files on a bunch of machines.

Because of these benefits, RPZ has become an essential tool for anyone wanting a secure and efficient DNS infrastructure.

WHAT WILL THIS BOOK COVER?

In this book "Advanced DNS Concepts: Response Policy Zones (RPZ)", we will learn more about RPZ:

- Chapter 2 refreshes your memory on basic DNS concepts needed for understanding RPZ.

- Chapter 3 offers a detailed look into what Response Policy Zones are.

- Chapter 4 guides you through setting up your own Response Policy Zone.

- Chapter 5 shares strategies for managing and solving common problems related to RPZ.

- Chapter 6 discusses how you can use RPZ for threat intelligence.

- Chapter 7 talks about common issues encountered during implementation.

- Chapter 8 provides some solutions to those pitfalls.

By the end of this book, not only will you know what makes up an RPZ but also how to create one yourself while avoiding some common challenges along the way.

Let's start our journey towards mastering advanced aspects of DNS technology with Response Policy Zones!

DNS REFRESHER

Before we delve deeper into Response Policy Zones (RPZ), let's refresh our knowledge on some essential DNS (Domain Name System) concepts that relate to RPZ.

CORE DNS CONCEPTS RELEVANT TO RPZ

DNS is like the phonebook of the internet. It translates human-friendly website names, such as www.example.com, into machine-friendly IP addresses, like 203.0.113.24, that computers use to communicate with each other. When you type a website name into your browser, it sends a query to a DNS server asking for the IP address associated with that name.

There are various parts involved in this process:

- DNS Resolver: This is the first stop in the DNS query process. It's typically provided by your Internet Service Provider (ISP), or, if you're in a corporate network, private infrastructure. (Or the rack next to your desk at home, if you're like me.)

- Root Servers: These servers respond where to find information about top-level domains (TLD) such as .com, .net, .us, and .example.

- TLD Servers: The root servers then direct the queries to servers responsible for specific domains. The authoritative DNS servers administrators give when they register a domain are configured here.

- Authoritative DNS Server: These servers provide the answer to your original query.

Understanding DNS Resolution and Responses

When you try to get to something on the Internet using a name, instead of an IP Address, you initiate a series of queries and responses between various servers - from resolver to root server to TLD server and finally authoritative server - until the desired IP address is found.

This entire process is known as "DNS resolution" and there are two basic ways to navigate distributed databases - find it yourself or ask someone else to do the work for you[2].

- Recursion/Recursive Server: The server you ask holds your query while it either checks its cache or goes to other servers to get the answer. When it has an answer from the other server, it gives that to you.

- Referral/Iterative Server: If the server you ask is not able to answer your query, it says, "I'm sorry; I don't the answer, but you can try this server to see if it knows." It then gives you the name servers responsible for that namespace or the root servers.

Once you reach the authoritative server for your query, you'll get a response. The response can take several forms:

- A positive answer if everything goes well.
- An NXDOMAIN response if no record exists for queried name.
- A SERVFAIL message if there was an error processing request.

If the response is an IP Address, yay, you're done. If get back another name, though, it triggers another lookup. This repeats until an IP Address is returned or someone gives up because it's taking too long to get an answer.

Importance of Security Measures within DNS

---

[2] These two approaches to resolution are outlined in RFC 1034.

Despite its vital role in internet navigation, traditional DNS has been designed without inherent security measures. Considering the standard was written in the 1980s, it's not surprising, but it does leave it vulnerable to numerous types of attacks like cache poisoning or DDoS attacks.

It's crucial that we implement security measures within our DNS infrastructure:

- DNSSEC[3] validates responses using digital signatures.
- RRL[4] limits rate at which responses are sent.
- RPZ allows us control over how our servers respond based on set policies.

These tools help ensure our online communications remain secure and reliable while preventing unauthorized access or damage to our network resources.

In our next chapter we'll dive deeper into Response Policy Zones and see how they provide added layer of control over traffic flowing through our network - enhancing security while optimizing performance.

---

[3] DNSSEC: Also known as DNS Security Extensions, DNSSEC adds an extra layer of security to the traditional DNS system. It achieves this by validating responses using digital signatures. This means when you get a response from a DNS query, DNSSEC helps ensure that it's from a trusted source and hasn't been tampered with during transit.

[4] RRL: Short for Response Rate Limiting, RRL is a technique used to control the rate at which responses are sent from a DNS server. By limiting the number of responses, RRL helps protect against certain types of attacks where an attacker tries to overwhelm a server with excessive requests - often referred to as DDoS attacks.

DEEP DIVE INTO RESPONSE POLICY ZONES

Now that we've recapped DNS basics and highlighted the importance of security within DNS infrastructure, it's time to learn more about our main topic - Response Policy Zones (RPZ).

DETAILED UNDERSTANDING OF RPZ CONCEPT

Response Policy Zones began as an experimental feature by the Internet Systems Consortium (ISC) in their DNS software, BIND, starting with version 9.8.1 in 2010. Several other DNS implementations support RPZ, including Unbound, PowerDNS, Knot DNS, Cisco Prime Network Registrar, and F5's BIG-IP.

Essentially, you can think of an RPZ as a special kind of zone file in your DNS server. But instead of containing information about domain names and IP addresses like a standard zone file, an RPZ contains "policy rules". These rules tell the server how to respond when it receives queries matching specific criteria such as client IP address or requested domain name.

For example, you could create a rule in your RPZ that tells your DNS server to return an NXDOMAIN response whenever it gets a query for badsite.example[5]. This means any user who tries to visit http:// badsite.example would get a 'page not found' error.

---

[5] The top level domain .example is reserved in RFC 2606. It's used here as a reminder that new global TLDs were introduced in 2013 and act just like the traditional .com, .org, and .net domains.

POLICY TRIGGERS AND ACTIONS

RPZ use two primary components to enforce rules: policy triggers and actions. These elements work together like a cause-and-effect mechanism within the system.

Policy triggers are the 'cause' in this scenario. They can be specific domain names or IP addresses that initiate an action when encountered during a DNS query. For instance, if there is a known malicious website or IP address, it can be set up as a policy trigger.

Once a trigger is identified, an action - the 'effect' - is activated. Actions dictate how the system should respond when it encounters a predetermined trigger. This can range from blocking access to redirecting traffic towards a different destination or even returning no data at all for that particular query.

For example, if we have identified "maliciouswebsite.invalid" as a potential threat and set it as our policy trigger, we could set our action to block any queries made to this domain. This means whenever this site is queried, our RPZ will intervene and prevent resolution, effectively blocking access.

It is important to note that RPZ is not a true firewall and will not prevent users from accessing a site directly by IP Address.

The power of RPZ lies in its flexibility and dynamic nature. It allows network administrators to customize their security measures according to their unique needs and concerns. By strategically defining policy triggers and actions, they can create an effective shield against potential threats.

MANAGE TRAFFIC AND ENHANCE SECURITY

With cyber threats becoming more complex and sophisticated, the need for tools like RPZ is greater than ever. By allowing admins to set custom policies for dealing with different types of queries, RPZ provide two primary benefits:

- **Improved Network Performance:** By directing traffic away from congested routes or towards preferred servers using policy rules, admins can optimize network performance.

- **Enhanced Security:** Admins can use policy rules to block access to known malicious domains or redirect suspicious traffic—thus improving security.

OVERRIDE SINGLE RECORDS FOR GRANULAR CONTROL

Manually overriding single records using Response Policy Zones is an incredibly powerful feature. It allows network administrators to have granular control over DNS responses without having to modify the original zone files or disrupt the overall structure of the domain.

When we say "overriding single records", we're essentially referring to manipulating the response a DNS server provides for specific queries. Instead of returning the IP address normally associated with a queried domain name (as defined in the original zone file), an RPZ can be configured to provide a different response based on predefined policy rules.

This is the same approach, but used for a slightly different purpose.

REAL-WORLD EXAMPLES

Let's look at some real-world examples where implementing RPZ can be beneficial:

Case 1: Blocking Malicious Domains: Suppose you know about a list of domains associated with malware or phishing attempts, such as micr0soft.invalid. You could use an RPZ to block these domains by creating policy rules that return NXDOMAIN responses for queries matching these domains.

Case 2: Blocking Specific Subdomains: Let's say there's a subdomain under your main domain involved in suspicious activities - suspicious.example.com. You can use an RPZ to specifically block access to this subdomain while letting other parts of your website function normally. You'll just need to set up a policy rule that provides NXDOMAIN response for queries matching suspicious.example.com.

Case 3: Redirecting Traffic: Let's say you have two servers - one that's overworked and another underutilized. You could create policy rules that redirect some traffic from the busy server towards the underutilized server - thus balancing load between them.

Case 4: Implementing Geographic Restrictions: If you want users from certain geographical regions not accessing certain content due to legal reasons, you could use an RPZ to implement these restrictions by creating policy rules based on client IP addresses.

Case 5: Overriding Single Records: Suppose you have a site - www.example.com - but due to some maintenance work, you temporarily want all traffic directed towards www.maintenance.example.com. Instead of changing your main zone file (which could be time-consuming and error-prone), you could use an RPZ to override this single record.

To achieve this, you'd create a policy rule within your RPZ that matches queries for www.example.com and returns the IP address for www.maintenance.example.com. As a result, any user trying to visit http://www.example.com would automatically be directed towards http://www.maintenance.example.com.

This approach is beneficial as it provides flexibility in managing traffic flow without needing to modify original DNS records. Also, once the maintenance work is over, simply removing or disabling this policy rule in your RPZ will restore the original routing.

As we continue our exploration into advanced DNS concepts, remember that each tool - including Response Policy Zones - may not be a one-size-fits-all solution but rather part of a broader strategy aimed at enhancing overall security and performance.

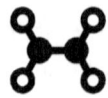

SETTING UP A RESPONSE POLICY ZONE

Now that we have an in-depth understanding of Response Policy Zones and the different ways they can be used, let's learn how to setup one. This chapter will guide you through the technical steps involved, discuss the role of policy triggers and actions, and share some best practices.

TECHNICAL STEPS INVOLVED IN SETTING UP AN RPZ

Setting up an RPZ requires planning, precise implementation, and thorough testing, regardless of your DNS server implementation. Here's an overview of steps involved using BIND:

1. **Prepare your DNS Server:** Ensure that your BIND version supports RPZ. If not, you will need to upgrade to a compatible version.

   Ideally, you should use a "bare metal" server - one that is not virtualized - because of the higher demands of the service.

2. **Define Your RPZ:** This is essentially creating a new zone file where you'll define your policy rules. Create a new file in the directory where your BIND configuration files reside, usually /etc/bind/. It is not important what you name this file, although it can helpful to use "RPZ" in it, such as rpz.local or rpzfirewall.db.

3. **Create Policy Rules:** Within this new zone file, start adding your policy rules - each having a trigger and corresponding action, which are shown

in more detail in the next section. The most common rule returns an NXDOMAIN response - the name doesn't exist:

```
badsite.example.com      CNAME .
```

Note that there is a period after the CNAME designation.

4. **Define RPZ Zone:** Add entries for your newly defined RPZ in named.conf or named.conf.options file with response-policy statement that points towards your newly created zone file (rpz.local or rpzfirewall.db).

```
zone "rpz" {
  type master;
  file "master/rpz.local";
    ...
};
```

Because an RPZ is configured like a valid zone (and, therefore, is one), it can be transferred between servers like any other zone.

5. **Enable RPZ Policies:** After defining your RPZ, you need to tell BIND about it by adding an entry in your named.conf or named.conf.options file - typically found in the same directory as the zone files. This involves adding a response-policy statement that points towards your newly created zone file (rpz.local). For example:

```
options {
  // other options here...
  response-policy { zone "rpz"; };
};
```

6. **Reload BIND Configuration:** After saving changes made to configuration files, you need to reload or restart the DNS service for changes to take effect.

Remember that these steps are general guidelines; specific procedures may vary based on factors such as operating system and network architecture.

Also note that working with sensitive files like BIND configurations requires appropriate permissions and careful handling – mistakes can lead to downtime or security issues.

THE ROLE OF POLICY TRIGGERS AND ACTIONS

As mentioned earlier, every policy rule within an RPZ consists of two parts: Trigger and Action.

Within BIND alone, the format of RPZs has changed several times, so verify which triggers and actions are valid with your DNS implementation and how to format them.

The Trigger defines when the rule should apply—it could be a specific domain name, subdomain, or IP Address. It's possible to match on the query or the response:

- Client IP Address
- QNAME or the query name
- Response IP Address
- NSDNAME or the name of the DNS server
- NSIP or the IP Address of the DNS server

The Action dictates what happens when that trigger is matched—it instructs DNS server how to respond.

- NXDOMAIN (CNAME .): The requested name does not exist.
- NODATA (CNAME *.): The name exists but there isn't a record for the type requested.
- PASSTHRU (CNAME rpz-passthru.): Overrides broader policies.
- DROP (CNAME rpz-drop.): Ignores the request and doesn't return anything.
- TCP-Only (CNAME rpz-tcp-only.): Forces a retry with TCP (used to mitigate reflection attacks).
- Local Data (arbitrary RR types): Returns the configured answer and not one of the special encoded responses.

For instance, if you want to block access to badsite.example, "badsite.example" will be your trigger and providing NXDOMAIN response will be your action.

Redirecting to an alternative domain: If you wish to redirect traffic from one domain to another, you could set up a policy rule with the original domain as the trigger and a CNAME record pointing towards the new domain as the Local Data action. For example:

oldwebsite.com CNAME newwebsite.com.

This rule instructs the DNS server to return the IP address of newwebsite.com whenever it gets queried for oldwebsite.com.

Returning a specific IP address: Perhaps there's a malicious website that you want to protect your users from accessing. You could set up a policy rule that returns an IP address of a warning page when the malicious website is queried:

example.invalid A 203.0.113.24

Here, 203.0.113.24[6] would be the IP of your warning page that informs users about potential threats.

Blocking access based on client's IP: RPZ can also use client IPs as triggers, which can be helpful in implementing geographic restrictions or blocking specific clients known for suspicious activities:

24.0.2.0.192.rpz-client-ip   CNAME   rpz-drop.

In this case, any DNS query coming from any client with an IP in the 192.0.2.0/24 network would be dropped without any response.

Understanding these components is crucial as they form the backbone of any RPZ setup - letting you control responses at granular level based on business need or security requirement.

---

[6] The address block 203.0.113.0/24 (TEST-NET-3) is reserved in RFC 5737.

BEST PRACTICES

While setting up an RPZ provides tremendous flexibility in managing DNS traffic flow and security measures, it's important to follow certain best practices:

- Plan Ahead: Before implementing any changes in live environment, carefully plan out which queries should trigger which responses - taking into account potential impact on users and operations.

- Ensure Interoperability: Some other DNS features, such as DNSSEC, may be incompatible or not work as expected.

- Test Thoroughly: Always test new configurations in isolated environments before deploying them live to ensure there are no unexpected disruptions.

- Document Changes: Keep track of all changes made within DNS setup. This provides valuable reference for troubleshooting future issues or audits.

- Stay Updated with Threat Intelligence Data: Regularly update your policy rules based on latest threat intelligence data to provide protection against evolving cyber threats.

Setting up an RPZ correctly and following best practices allows you to harness their true power, leading towards improved security and optimizing network performance.

MANAGEMENT AND MAINTENANCE

Response Policy Zones act as a shield against online dangers. But like any good defense system, we need to manage and maintain RPZ properly for them to work best.

Maintaining an Effective RPZ

Keeping an RPZ working well requires a plan that spots potential problems and sorts them out before they become big issues. This starts with creating clear rules about what triggers an action in your RPZ and regularly updating these rules as new threats appear.

- Keep current: A useful way to do this is by using automatic updates from trusted sources that keep track of risky websites or IP addresses. These can be added straight into your RPZ rules.

- Monitor the network: Regularly checking your network activity can help spot unusual patterns that might mean there's a threat, so tools that allow you to do this in real-time are really useful.

- Audit policies: Doing routine security checks is another good strategy. Regularly reviewing how effective your RPZ rules are ensures they're still doing their job correctly. This could involve checking if certain sites are being blocked as expected or if harmless sites have been mistakenly marked as dangerous.

TROUBLESHOOTING COMMON ISSUES

Even with the best plans, you might still run into some problems which will need fixing.

- **Poor performance:** One common problem is slower response times because the extra processing needed for. If this happens, you might need to tweak your rules or upgrade your system hardware.

- **False positives:** Another issue is when safe websites get blocked because of overly strict rules. In these cases, adjusting your triggers or creating an exceptions list for certain sites would help.

- **Missed threats:** On other occasions, dangerous sites may not be blocked even though they should be – this could happen if rule definitions aren't accurate or the information feeds are outdated. To fix this, make sure you're getting regular updates from reliable sources and check your rule definitions carefully.

- **Policy Conflicts:** If multiple policies are defined within the same Response Policy Zone, there might be conflicts or unexpected behavior depending on their order of precedence.

Taking care of an RPZ involves both planning ahead and reacting quickly - combining these strategies ensures a strong defense against ever-changing online threats. As we rely more on our digital networks, having these skills becomes crucial in keeping them safe.

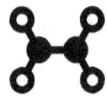

USING RPZ FOR THREAT INTELLIGENCE

In our online safety journey, we've discovered the power of Response Policy Zones. Now let's step up its effectiveness with something called threat feeds.

THE USE OF THREAT FEEDS

Threat feeds are like news updates or intelligence reports about dangerous places on the internet. They're lists of risky websites or IP addresses given to us by trusted sources that keep an eye on what's happening on the web and warn us about new threats.

Adding these threat feeds to your RPZ makes it work even better. Instead of you having to search for new dangers on the web and update your rules, these feeds do most of this work for you. They keep your RPZ filled with fresh information about harmful sites so it can stop them before they cause any problems.

ADDING THREAT INTELLIGENCE FEEDS INTO YOUR SYSTEM

Knowing how important these threat feeds are is key; next, we'll look at how to add them into your current setup smoothly.

- Choose trustworthy sources for your threat feeds: There are lots of choices out there, so it's really important to go for ones known for their top-quality work. Remember, the better the source quality, the better your security!

Threat Intelligence Platforms (TIPs) allow you to combine multiple feeds into one, simplifying administration.

- **Add the feed to your configuration:** Once you've subscribed, you should be given the URL for the feed or some other way of accessing it. If your provider doesn't have an automated way of updating the feed on your system, you will need to periodically update your data.

- **Schedule updates:** For those dealing with many networks or lots of traffic, you'll have to decide where best to put in these updates and how often they should happen. You can stagger them across different parts of your network to keep from updating everything at the same time or schedule during off-peak times when there's less traffic.

- **Prioritize:** Another good move is deciding which threats get added first based on risk levels – this makes sure serious threats get blocked right away while less urgent ones can wait, if needed.

Using an RPZ with threat intelligence gives us a really strong shield against online dangers. By picking top-quality threat feeds and adding them smoothly into our system, we create a defense that stays updated against new threats without needing constant manual changes. As we spend more time in our digital world where risks can change quickly and without warning, having this automatic shield becomes more important than ever in keeping our networks safe.

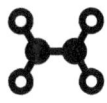

COMMON PITFALLS

Our journey into online safety might run into some hazards along way. As we consider some of these common challenges, keep in mind that for every problem, there is a solution. So let's explore these pitfalls before we see how we can overcome them in the next chapter.

SELECTING RELIABLE THREAT FEEDS

With so many options out there it can be hard to know which ones will give you the best quality data. Choosing the wrong ones could leave your network open to threats that better quality feeds would have caught.

Quality of Data: Not all threat feeds are created equal. Some might provide comprehensive and highly accurate data, while others may have a higher rate of false positives or outdated information.

Timeliness of Updates: Threat landscapes evolve rapidly, so it's critical that threat feeds are updated frequently to provide the most current information about potential threats.

Relevance: The feed should be relevant to your specific needs and environment. For instance, if you're mainly concerned with protecting against phishing attempts, then a feed focused on malware might not be as useful.

Cost: Some high-quality threat feeds can be costly, which could be prohibitive especially for smaller organizations.

Ease of Integration: The selected RPZ feed must be compatible with your DNS system and easy to integrate into your existing security architecture.

Vendor Reputation and Support: It's crucial to choose a vendor that's reputable and offers good customer support in case issues arise during integration or usage of the feed.

Managing Updates

If you're dealing with large networks or high traffic volumes, figuring out when and where to implement updates without slowing everything down can be tricky.

Operational Overhead/Lack of Automation: Regularly updating RPZs requires time and resources, which can be labor-intensive and prone to delays or inconsistencies. This can be significant in larger environments.

Compatibility Issues: Updates may be incompatible with certain system configurations or other DNS features, leading to potential operational issues.

Performance Impact: Updating RPZ records might temporarily impact DNS server performance, potentially causing slower response times.

Risk of Errors: Manual updates increase the risk of human error, which could cause operational disruptions or leave systems vulnerable to threats.

Synchronization Challenges: In a distributed system with multiple DNS servers, synchronizing RPZ updates across all servers can be complex.

Disruption to Legitimate Traffic: If an update includes incorrect entries (false positives), it could end up blocking legitimate traffic, affecting business operations until the issue is resolved.

Inadequate Testing Environment: Without proper testing environment set up for RPZ updates, there's a risk of deploying unverified changes that could disrupt normal operations if they don't function as expected.

Resource Limitations: Depending on hardware capacity and network infrastructure, managing numerous large-scale threat feeds and processing them in real-time could exceed resource capabilities.

CREATING EFFECTIVE POLICIES

It might seem like a good idea to block as much as possible but this can lead to over blocking - where safe sites get blocked along with the risky ones because the rules are too strict - or under blocking - where too many risky sites are allowed.

Understanding Threat Landscape: A fundamental challenge is understanding the nature of threats your organization faces, as this affects what kind of policies you need to implement.

Balancing Security and Accessibility: Striking the right balance between security and accessibility is difficult. Overly strict policies might block legitimate traffic (false positives), while too lax ones could let threats slip through.

Keeping Policies Up-to-Date: As new threats emerge, old ones evolve, or your organization's tolerance to risk changes, your RPZ policies will need to be updated accordingly. This requires continuous effort and vigilance.

Policy Complexity: Depending on the size and complexity of your network infrastructure, creating and managing a large number of policy rules can be challenging.

Resource Constraints: Implementing comprehensive RPZ policies may require substantial computational resources, especially in large-scale environments that deal with high volumes of DNS queries.

Inadequate Expertise: Crafting effective RPZ policies requires a deep understanding of DNS operations and threat intelligence, which might not always be available within an organization's IT team.

Compliance Requirements: Some organizations operate under regulatory mandates that dictate specific security measures or restrict certain practices, adding another layer of complexity to policy creation.

Risk Assessment Difficulties: Identifying the level of risk associated with different types of accesses or threats can be complex but is crucial for setting appropriate response rules in the RPZ policy.

While the challenges can seem daunting, there are a lot of possible solutions available to us. Let's keep traveling.

MITIGATION STRATEGIES

The final stop on our journey lets us look at some of the ideas available to deal with threat feed selection, staying current, and creating policies that do what you want (and don't do what you don't want!)

SELECTING RELIABLE THREAT FEEDS

When selecting a threat feed, it's important to do thorough research, consider taking advantage of trial periods or sample data sets provided by vendors, and continuously monitor the effectiveness of chosen feeds once implemented.

Evaluate Data Quality: Before subscribing to a threat feed, do a thorough evaluation of the quality of data it provides. This could involve reviewing sample data sets, checking for false positives or negatives, and comparing with other feeds if possible.

Ensure Frequent Updates: Choose feeds that are updated frequently to ensure you're protecting against the most recent threats. The feed provider should provide information about how often their data is updated.

Choose Relevant Feeds: Make sure to choose feeds that are relevant to your specific needs and threats your organization faces. For instance, if you're a financial institution, prioritize those that provide information about threats related to banking and finance.

Consider Cost-Effectiveness: While cost shouldn't be the only factor in choosing a threat feed, it's important to consider whether a particular feed offers value for its price.

Test Integration: Before committing to a specific feed, test how easily it integrates into your existing security infrastructure. This will help avoid issues down the line.

Research Vendor Reputation and Support: Do some research on the reputation of the vendor providing the feed as well as their customer support services. A reputable vendor with good support can make all the difference when issues arise.

Monitor for Over/Under Blocking: Regularly review your DNS query logs for any signs of over blocking or under blocking based on your threat feeds and adjust accordingly.

Use Multiple Feeds: Using multiple threat feeds can help improve accuracy and coverage by cross-verifying threats among different sources.

Continuously Review Effectiveness: Once implemented, continuously monitor the effectiveness of chosen feeds and make adjustments as necessary based on changing needs or observed performance.

Remember that no solution is perfect – there will always be trade-offs – but these steps can help increase your chances of selecting a reliable RPZ threat feed that meets your organization's needs.

Managing Updates

To make managing updates easier, it's important to use automation, keep a close watch on things and check them regularly, test thoroughly before starting, and train your staff properly.

Implement Automation: Minimize operational overhead and reduce the risk of human error by automating as much of the update process as possible. This could involve using scripts or software tools to automatically download and apply updates from your threat feed provider.

Use a Centralized Management System: If you have multiple DNS servers, consider using a centralized DNS management system. This allows you to manage all your RPZ configurations from one place, making it easier to distribute updates across your network.

Schedule Updates Strategically: Schedule updates during off-peak times to minimize potential impacts on network performance.

Create a Testing Environment: Before applying updates to your live environment, test them in a controlled setting first. This can help identify any potential issues before they can affect your operations.

Monitor & Audit Regularly: Regular monitoring and auditing of your DNS servers can help identify any issues with updates early, allowing you to fix them quickly before they cause disruptions.

Quality Threat Feed Selection: Ensure that the threat feeds being used are reliable and up-to-date to effectively address threats while minimizing false positives/negatives.

Consider Redundancy & Failover Planning: Having backup servers ready for failover can mitigate downtime risks during an update or if an error occurs post-update.

Proper Training of IT Staff: Ensure that those responsible for managing RPZ updates are adequately trained on the process and understand how to troubleshoot common issues that may arise during this task.

Optimize Resource Usage: Properly plan server capacity based on the size and frequency of threat feed data ingestion and processing needs.

By implementing these strategies, you can effectively manage their RPZ updates despite the inherent challenges you might encounter along the way.

Creating Effective Policies

Writing policies with the correct syntax is easy; writing effective policies requires training, ongoing review, and the use of tools where it makes sense.

Expand Threat Knowledge: Regularly update your understanding of the current threat landscape. This can be achieved by subscribing to relevant security newsletters, attending security seminars, or even hiring a dedicated security analyst.

Balance Security and Accessibility: Create policies that strike a balance between blocking malicious traffic and allowing legitimate traffic. Regularly monitor and adjust policies as needed to maintain this balance.

Continuous Policy Updates: Stay ahead of evolving threats by regularly updating your RPZ policies based on new threat intelligence or changes in your organization's risk tolerance.

Simplify Policies Where Possible: Use tools or strategies to manage complex policy rules efficiently such as group-based policies, wildcard entries, and automated policy management tools.

Allocate Adequate Resources: Ensure you have enough computational resources to implement comprehensive RPZ policies, especially if you're dealing with high volumes of DNS queries.

Invest in Training or Hiring Expertise: Consider investing in additional training for your IT team on DNS operations and threat intelligence or hire external experts if necessary.

Ensure Compliance: Keep abreast of any regulatory requirements affecting your organization and ensure these are incorporated into your RPZ policy creation process.

Conduct Regular Risk Assessments: Regularly assess the risks associated with different types of accesses or threats to set appropriate response rules in the RPZ policy.

Implement Monitoring Tools: Deploy monitoring solutions that provide visibility into how well your RPZs are performing and whether they're effectively blocking intended threats without interrupting legitimate traffic.

Create an Incident Response Plan: Even with the best-laid plans, incidents may occur - having a response plan will ensure that when they do happen, they can be managed quickly and effectively minimizing potential damage.

While implementing an RPZ does come with its own set of challenges, they're all manageable with careful planning and smart strategies. Whether it's selecting top-quality threat feeds, planning how best to manage updates without disruption, or setting up balanced RPZ rules that effectively guard against threats without unnecessary over blocking, each pitfall has a solution waiting to be found.

CONCLUSION

I hope "Advanced DNS Concepts: Response Policy Zones (RPZ)" has served as a comprehensive, but only slightly boring, guide to understanding and implementing RPZ.

We began by revisiting basic DNS concepts to lay the groundwork for our exploration into RPZ. Detailed insights were provided on their structure and function, along with practical guidance on setting up your own RPZ. Solutions were discussed for common issues encountered, equipping you with valuable tools to manage and resolve these challenges effectively. Moreover, we delved into the potential of RPZ for threat intelligence, opening new avenues for security enhancements.

As we close this book, it's important to remember that mastery comes with practice and persistence. The knowledge acquired here should serve as a solid foundation from which you can confidently create and manage your own Response Policy Zones. Ultimately, this is but one step in a broader journey towards DNS mastery.

Don't forget to stop to smell the flowers!

RESOURCES/REFERENCES

1. Consortium, I. S. (2021, May 26). Response Policy Zones (RPZ). https://www.isc.org/rpz/

2. Vixie, P., & Schryver, V. (2013). DNS Response Policy Zones (DNS RPZ). IETF Datatracker. https://datatracker.ietf.org/doc/draft-vixie-dnsop-dns-rpz/00/

3. Eastlake 3rd, D., & Panitz, A. (1999, June). Reserved Top Level DNS Names. RFC 2606. https://tools.ietf.org/html/rfc2606

4. Arkko, J., Cotton, M., & Vegoda, L. (2010, January). IPv4 Address Blocks Reserved for Documentation. RFC 5737. https://tools.ietf.org/html/rfc5737

5. IANA IPV4 Special-Purpose Address Registry. (n.d.). https://www.iana.org/assignments/iana-ipv4-special-registry/iana-ipv4-special-registry.xhtml

6. Mockapetris, P. (1987, November). Domain names - concepts and facilities. RFC 1034. https://tools.ietf.org/html/rfc1034

7. Ruberg, B. (2015, December 8). Overriding DNS for fun and profit. / Techblog. https://www.redpill-linpro.com/techblog/2015/12/08/dns-rpz.html

8. Unbound - about. (n.d.). NLnet Labs. https://nlnetlabs.nl/projects/unbound/about/

9. Home. (n.d.). https://www.powerdns.com/

10. Knot DNS. (n.d.). https://www.knot-dns.cz/

11. Cisco Prime Network Registrar. (2022, November 16). Cisco. https://www.cisco.com/c/en/us/products/cloud-systems-management/prime-network-registrar/index.html

12. BIG-IP DNS. (n.d.). F5, Inc. https://www.f5.com/products/big-ip-services/big-ip-dns